D.A.T.E. READY

Daughters After Truth Everyday

Surrendering to Freedom

Corinna Smith

D.A.T.E. READY | Daughters After Truth Everyday Surrendering To Freedom. Copyright © 2020. Corinna Smith.

Published by:

DAYELight
PUBLISHERS

ISBN: 978-1-949343-66-3 (paperback)

Scripture quotations marked KJV are from the King James Version of the Bible.

Scripture quotations marked NKJV are taken from the New King James Version®. Copyright © 1982 by Thomas Nelson. Used by permission. All rights reserved.

Scripture quotations marked NLT are taken from the *Holy Bible*, New Living Translation, copyright © 1996, 2004, 2015 by Tyndale House Foundation. Used by permission of Tyndale House Publishers, Inc., Carol Stream, Illinois 60188. All rights reserved.

Scripture quotations marked CSB are from The Christian Standard Bible. Copyright © 2017 by Holman Bible Publishers. Used by permission. Christian Standard Bible®, and CSB® are federally registered trademarks of Holman Bible Publishers, all rights reserved.

Cover photo taken by Niketa Pechan (Keta Christine Visuals)

TABLE OF CONTENTS

Acknowledgements

Writing this book was one of the hardest assignments I've had to complete! Not that the writing was hard but revisiting some of these seasons of my life was a process! I would first like to thank God for just being such an awesome Father and seeing in me what I didn't! For loving me when I didn't love myself, and for walking with me and transforming my life. I'm forever grateful! I could never repay You but I'll spend the rest of my life giving you what you deserve, glory!

To my children: Tyreke, Teleke, & Taliyah Lockhart I love you all so much. You all push mommy to grow and it is a delight being your mom. You make me so proud and help me to grow and I have seen amazing strength that I didn't know I possessed because of you all!

To my spiritual mom Olga Claxton, thank you for allowing God to use you to correct and teach me many things He has had you to impart in me that are still lasting and for pushing me to obey God in my purpose.

To my spiritual fathers Warren Claxton, Darryl Auberry, and Rudolph Barber I am forever grateful for all of you for not counting it robbery to sow the word of God faithfully and showing me the true love of a Father. For the counseling, encouragement, and consistently being there for me I'm so thankful.

To my natural mom Lavonda Smith I love you dearly and I know God knew what He was doing when He chose you for the task to be my mom, you have helped me grow in love greatly! Thank you for the love that you show to my children and I and being there whenever we need you, you are appreciated.

To my Jonathan and David covenant partner June McCalla (and her head my brother Kevin McCalla) thank you both so much for your labor of love. God knows how special I feel that He gave me your friendship, you have truly walked in the trenches with me and truly showed me the love of Christ! Many people have come and gone but I'm so grateful that you remained.

To my close friends, my inner circle, my confidants and accountability partners, I love you all so much. The bond we share can't be replaced.

To my editor and sister Deborah Johnson thank you for all the encouragement over the years and being an example of virtue and strength. Thank you for helping to see this assignment to its completion, you are beautiful inside and out.

To one of my midwives Patricia Joseph, sis I love you so much! You may not realize it but you are so special to me and such a great supporter and friend. I will never forget the night you sat with me until 3 am as DATE Ready was birthed.

To all my FireStarter International sisters, it's too many of you to name, I love you all so much! Thank you for the encouragement, prayers, phone calls, reminders to keep writing, hugs, and love. You all challenge me greatly and you all push me to be who God has called me to be.

To my publisher Crystal Daye of Daye Light Publishing thank you for all your help birthing this book into the earth. Getting your regular emails gave me such inspiration to complete the task.

To my church, One Body in Christ in Love, thank you all for being such a loving and supportive family. I have felt at home since the first day I walked through the doors, I love you all.

To the brethren abroad who have showed so much love over the years, even if we may not talk often now, I'm still so grateful for you all. It's so many who have played a role and are significant so even if I didn't mention your name specifically, I share my gratitude and love for you!

INTRODUCTION

Let me tell you about a man who told me everything about me! This is NOT the story about the woman at the well, but about a woman who like her, encountered a love that exposed and continues to expose every hidden place. This love healed wounds and stretched me in ways that I thought weren't possible. That man's name is Jesus the Christ, the Son of the Living God, and since I encountered Him, I have never been the same. However, before I can tell of the many things the Lord has done for me and in me, I have to take you back to where it all started.

Chapter 1
IN THE BEGINNING

I was born on November 16, 1985 to my mother and father who were a young married couple at the time. I was the youngest of five children to my mother, as well as the youngest of my father, who had three children. My childhood can be explained as a summary of memories, some vague and others that seemed to haunt me even up to adulthood. Although my parents were married and together at the time of my birth they were separated soon after. My father was a great provider at the time, but later that turned into a cycle of drug abuse and eventually my mom followed. I don't remember much from that time being that I was so young, but over the years I was told many stories that usually line up no matter the narrator. I grew up like most kids who are born into broken families, some normal days mixed in with chaos, hurt, pain, and anger, resulting in brokenness.

Once God's order is removed out of a situation the product of that becomes what our society looks like today. As a toddler, I was removed from the custody of my mother. My sister and I lived with my grandmother on my Father's side. I loved my grandmother so much, and I'll never forget the day I was called out of class in middle school to hear that she was on her way out of my earthly life for good. It was one of the most devastating things that I have endured in my life because my grandmother was the one person that I never questioned her love for me. I knew I was loved by others, like my parents but I can honestly say I never questioned her love for me. I used to talk to her about things that I couldn't talk to others about. It's like she understood me in a way that no one else did until I began my relationship with Christ of course. I trusted her and I knew she was someone that I could depend on to be there for me even if I was forsaken by all others. Now, in reality, she also suffered from alcohol abuse, and though my testimony of her is loving, that may not be the testimony of others. She like every other human being had flaws, was hurt and hurt others. Nonetheless, I loved her, and I knew she loved me.

Eventually, my mom recovered from the addiction and worked her butt off to regain custody of her children — my sister and I being the first of the redeemed. This is normally how most fairytale stories begin — the abandoned children regained by the loving parents — but unfortunately for me, it was the beginning of one of the most traumatic experiences of my life.

Chapter 2
THE TRAUMA

After years of settling back into this re-established home setting, another sibling was granted access back home as well. During his time of separation, he had the misfortune of being inserted in the foster care system, where I later learned that doors of sexual abuse were opened into his life, and in turn, he began to open them to mine as well. I don't even remember how long it went on, but I will say that though I have memories the Lord was gracious to blot out a lot of it and that part I am grateful for. I know to most that sounds crazy, but for those who can relate, we know that some things are better left unremembered. I must say that whether the full detail memories remain or not, in Christ He makes all things new.

> *And he that sat upon the throne said, Behold, I make all things new. And he said unto me, Write: for these words are true and faithful.*
> *—Revelation 21:5 (NKJV)*

When the love of God gets a hold of you and you become a new creation, you learn that no matter your past or what you have encountered or experienced in life you can move forward in love, and love Himself (God) will teach you how to forgive and love those who have hurt you. I have to also add that God has built and restored my relationship with my brother and even with my mom in a way that I didn't believe was possible. Before getting to this place I spent years holding on to anger and bitterness from what I endured as a child. I even went through a season after receiving Christ of convincing myself that I had forgiven them, but I never truly let Christ deal with it!

There are some people who believe that when something has taken place from such a long time ago, it should just be buried and left alone, but that's not how the Heavenly Father deals with things. Yes, it's from the past, but there comes a time when you have to confront the past and acknowledge it because without doing so, no true healing can take place. This is even true with salvation; how can our sins be forgiven, and we be transformed if we don't acknowledge that we have erred from God's way? It's impossible! I've also observed that amongst the African American culture, there is a tendency to try to bury these types of situations because they were taught, "What goes on in this house stays in this house." The problem with that is, without talking about or ever addressing these things, the victims and the offender never truly get a chance to recover. That's why we see so many adults walking around bleeding from old hurts and the residue leaks out in everything they do! For some, this looks like anger and outbursts of wrath, aggression for others, and for some promiscuity and cycles of bad relationships, etc.

I know there are some who even say, "If God is Sovereign, why does He sit back and allow these things to happen?" I would simply answer that He is Sovereign, but He gives mankind free will, and unfortunately, with that will comes the choice to choose what displeases Him. What kind of God would He be anyway if He forced us to love Him or do what He says? I am a witness that though this wasn't an ideal experience to endure, my Father has the ability to give beauty for ashes and turn messes into messages. It's beautiful to see God make such a loving friendship between individuals who the enemy wanted to engraft with hatred towards one another. Although what my brother did to me was the beginning, it was certainly not the end. Other doors of perversion began opening in my life, like pornography, homosexuality, masturbation, other acts of incest, and so on. My brother didn't live with us long after I ended up confiding in my grandmother about the abuse, but even after he moved out of the home, there was still another door to perversion left still residing in the home.

> *Therefore if any man be in Christ, he is a new creature: old things are passed away; behold, all things are become new.*
> *—2 Corinthians 5:17 (KJV)*

Chapter 3
OPEN DOORS

Being a mother myself now and being awakened in the knowledge of God, I understand that these doors of perversion usually start with us. I'm sure that my mom didn't know that living in the home unmarried with her boyfriend was a door all by itself. I know this may challenge some of the beliefs of the readers right now, but perversion is simply taking something outside of the context of which it was designed to be used. So, being that God is Creator and was the One who established what relationships looked like from the very beginning — with one man and one woman in Holy matrimony — who are we as creation to decide that we can change it? That's the thing, we simply can't. We can't just choose to disobey and do things our own way because unfortunately, disobedience comes with consequences. When you have children, they take part in the suffering with you.

As adults, we take on the mindset that "I'm grown" and "I can do as I please, so do as I say and not as I do," but we have to understand that our greatest influence is what we do not just what we say! The other downfall is that whatever we expose ourselves to, we automatically expose our children to as well. In other words, as a mother you never have to bring a man around your children, you can meet him at his home, have sex with him there, and your children may never know; but you can't escape the fact that you have just connected yourself to another soul and have now taken on their demons and everything else they are dealing with. So guess what, you may leave him at his home, but he is still coming home with you, and everything that you may be trying to keep them from is now up close and personal and living with them. This is not just true in the spiritual sense but also in the natural. For example, if you have sex with someone with an STD, there's a great chance that what you expose yourself to, you may end up living with. Like a mother who contracts HIV from a partner and now her kids have to watch her slowly decay and go through the protocol of daily pills and sickness, hospital visits, and the thought of (and in some cases) the reality of her dying and leaving them for good. So let's be clear, we may be adults, but our choices affect other people; and just as mine altered the life of my children, my parent's choices altered mine.

It's interesting because it is usually in these times that we think that we are doing what's best for our loved ones. The enemy tries to get you to look at the pros of certain choices and though superficially it may seem to produce the best outcome, the one that matters the most has the greatest negative impact! I'm sure that no one intentionally opens the door to harm but there is a point where we have to take accountability for the doors that are opened indirectly. Let's make it simple, with every choice moving forward, someone's life and future could be altered. Consider that before you open the door of your life to the next relationship, job, friendship, marriage, etc. — especially as parents. I even make it a practice now to consider how my family, my children, the body of Christ, and those who God uses me to influence in any way would be affected by the choices I make. I'm learning that when you allow the word of God and the leading of the Holy Spirit to be your guide, the Lord will show you which doors to close and which to walk through!

Chapter 4
WHAT WE SEE MATTERS

My sister and I endured years of not being able to bathe or change clothes in peace for the fear of being watched. My mom didn't know at the time that what she had entangled herself with had an issue with his eyes. I describe it that way because we sometimes think what we look upon even in secret is innocent, such as pornography and even looking upon others with lust, but what we don't understand is that the eyes are an entryway to the heart.

> *I will set nothing wicked before my eyes;*
> *I hate the work of those who fall away;*
> *It shall not cling to me.*
> *A perverse heart shall depart from me;*
> *I will not know wickedness.*
> *—Psalm 101:3–4 (NKJV)*

What we see matters because what and how we see alters how we live and the things that we do; and when it comes to opening up the eye gate to perversion, be clear that the enemy does not stop there. It will start with the eye, but soon that won't satisfy, so sin begins to graduate to the next level and so on and before you know it, you find yourself looking back and asking how did I get here? I was exposed to magazines and videos as a child and grew up being addicted to both porn and masturbation because of what I saw! I would also say don't make excuses for this either because true freedom comes from acknowledging that it's wrong. Let me kill the lie now, every man doesn't watch porn, nor is every person overtaken by lust, so don't use that as an excuse to stay bound. Simply acknowledge that it's in you, and through your confession and repentance, God can deliver you from this!

> *Let no one say when he is tempted, "I am tempted by God"; for God cannot be tempted by evil, nor does He Himself tempt anyone. But each one is tempted when he is drawn away by his own desires and enticed. Then, when desire has conceived, it gives birth to sin; and sin, when it is full-grown, brings forth death.*
> *—James 1:13–15 (NKJV)*

It's interesting that this was actually one of the first things I was delivered from, I watched God literally take the desire away! This just wasn't a once delivered always delivered thing either, I fight daily to stay free! I am careful with what I look at on TV, the type of movies I see, and even the conversations that I partake in. The best thing is to be real with you! Be honest with yourself about your weaknesses, and I tell people this all the time — PUT NO CONFIDENCE IN YOUR FLESH (Philippians 3:3)!

At this point in my life, I was still a child, so there was not much that I could do, but my sister, being a little older, began to run away and enter a life of rebellion. And only she and God know the fullness of what she has endured and still hasn't mustered the courage to talk about yet. However, when she left, I was left to endure it alone.

Chapter 5
REGRET TO REPETITION

I remember times when I use to cry myself to sleep and wonder what I had done to be born into this type of reality. I made excellent grades being a straight "A" student almost all the way through grade school and didn't get into much trouble. But no matter how good I tried to be, I ended up dealing with a hand that I wouldn't have chosen for myself. I look back now, after making similar choices of those before me, and I know sometimes the thoughts that I felt then, my children may sometimes feel.

Unfortunately, my decisions have left my 3 children to be fatherless — not that their father is deceased — and to not be able to experience the full benefits of childhood with both parents as God designed for it to be. They've even had to endure my instability at times and emotional rollercoaster from relationship to relationship; times when I was present in body but emotionally and attentively so absent. It's funny because some of the time, I tried to convince myself that I was doing what was best for them by attempting to find someone to fulfill the role of father for them and husband for me, almost like trying to correct my previous mistakes.

The reality of the matter is that it wasn't helping at all. It was bad enough that my choice to not submit my body to God until marriage caused me to walk into single motherhood, but then I kept repeating those steps and brought different people in and out of our lives, which opened up their heart and emotions to people who God never intended to be a part of their life in that way. So when they ended up leaving, by my choice or theirs, the kids were left to pick up the broken heart pieces along with me. One thing I have learned is that only God can heal a broken heart, so choosing someone to attempt the task is only asking for trouble.

He heals the brokenhearted and binds up their wounds.
—Psalm 147:3 (NKJV)

It's also funny to me that though I knew the things that I had endured and didn't want my children to endure them as well, I was making choices that could have also put them in harm's way. By the grace of God, that didn't happen, but I was indulging in behaviors that it could have. Every solution that I was coming up with to be different were mere alterations of sin! I ended up becoming the very thing that I despised! Honestly, it wasn't until I rendered my heart to Him that I was truly able to focus on me and allow God to dig into those wounded places that I use to seek comfort from in others. I can look back and see that everything I sought refuge in was never meant to be a shelter for me but rather it was only meant to be found in Christ. We each have this God-sized hole in us that only the Lord can fill.

Chapter 6
SELF-SEEKING

I didn't see it then, but it all boiled down to me being selfish, seeking my own desires and what I wanted being more important than what they needed. See, I didn't understand then that a father figure to be present and help provide for them was only the minor detail of what they needed. They needed me first to be the mother to them that God created me to be — the one walking in the image and likeness of the King. Being the woman who, though she made mistakes, understood the path she walked previously didn't lead to victory, but rather the woman who allowed God to tear down the lies of the enemy and build her back upon an unshakable foundation. A foundation that's not based upon how pretty I am or the way my body looks, nor my credentials or salary, but solely based on the fact that I am a child of the God of all creation.

> *Love is patient and kind. Love is not jealous or boastful or proud or rude. It does not demand its own way. It is not irritable, and it keeps no record of being wronged.*
> *— 1 Corinthians 13:4–5 (NLT)*

As parents, it is second nature to love your children, right? Do you know that every time we consider our desires over the best interest of our children, we are not walking in love with them? We already know that they did not ask to be born, but since we took the initiative to bring them into the world, we have a God-given responsibility to do what's best for them. The first on the list being to train them up in the knowledge of the Lord! Self-seeking is defined as having concern for one's own welfare and interests before others or to be self-serving. Consider that before lust, your desires, or what you think you need causes you to lean in a direction that is only fitting for you! Even if you are not a parent, you have a level of influence that is important in someone's life! Take them into consideration in your decision-making process, there are people who look up to you that you may not even be aware of. If you must be self-seeking, seek to learn who you truly are in Christ and what identity in Him means for you!

> *Do nothing out of selfish ambition or conceit, but in humility consider others as more important than yourselves. Everyone should look out not only for his own interests, but also for the interests of others.*
> *—Philippians 2:3–4 (CSB)*

Chapter 7
IDENTITY

I had to learn that I bought into the lie that a man was what was missing from my idea of what a family is supposed to be when in actuality, TRUTH is what was missing — the truth about who I was and what I really needed! At that time my identity was wrapped in the idea of what material possessions I had and how I could achieve things that I thought would make me complete, like marriage or a degree. I was basically consumed in pursuing the idols of my heart.

It's ironic that we make this list in our minds of the things that we think we need, and our God is so sovereign that HE will allow us to achieve some of them, only to let us see that life doesn't consist in those things. You would think that one failed relationship after the other would be the sounding alarm in someone's mind to know that it's not the missing link, but unfortunately, for most in darkness, we are too blind to see it! The truth is, you can achieve that goal or get that thing or that relationship on your own, but if you don't have Christ as Lord and Savior, and Holy Spirit indwelling, you will still be empty, still discontent, and attempting to achieve more! A sure way to know that this is your issue is that internal thought that says, "When I get this, or when I achieve that I will be happy!" Don't believe the lie, true contentment is found in Christ!

Then he said, "Beware! Guard against every kind of greed. Life is not measured by how much you own."
—Luke 12:15 (NLT)

Now godliness with contentment is great gain.
—1 Timothy 6:6 (NKJV)

Can I interject right here and say that it is in not knowing your true identity that the root of this issue lies! As mankind, we were created to be in the image and likeness of God; the reason why we aren't doing what we were created to do is that somewhere along the way, we lost what that image should truly look like. We often look to the world and the things and people around us to guide us on how we should mold our lives. We let the media direct us on what is good and acceptable, forgetting that we were already given the parameters to be successful in this life. Those instructions come from the word of God (Holy Bible), and if you already have an image of who you are without it, you are truly missing out on the fullness that has been predestined for your life.

But you are a chosen generation, a royal priesthood, a holy nation, His own special people, that you may proclaim the praises of Him who called you out of darkness into His marvelous light;
—1 Peter 2:9 (NKJV)

But as many as received Him, to them He gave the right to become children of God, to those who believe in His name.
—John 1:12

In this life, I wear many hats. I am a mother, a hairstylist, a friend, a minister of the gospel, a poet, and an author. But none of these roles could ever compare to simply being His daughter! There is peace and solace that comes with having your identity wrapped in being His own, especially considering the price that was paid to even make it possible — His life. I know that nothing that I've ever done is deserving of the love and fellowship that is extended through Christ, yet it is graciously given to me. All hell could literally be breaking loose in my life, and simply reflecting on the fact that I am loved, I am accepted, and my Father is in control, puts everything in its perspective. It is also for this very cause that my life has been transformed.

I no longer feel like an orphan or unwanted, I am fully persuaded that I am absolutely loved by the Father. It is with this mindset that I also know that because of Who I now belong to I can't just behave any type of way or do whatever I want, I have the objective to please and serve my Heavenly Father. It matters to me now how I represent Him and how people may view Him because of me, so I allow His word to guide me. I spend time with Him in prayer, worship and praise, and in His word so that I can know His heart and how He views and feels about life. It's simple, I am not my own, I belong to Him and because that is my identity no one can come along and convince me to turn away.

Chapter 8
SURRENDER TO SUBSTITUTION

The first attempt I made to surrender my ideology that a relationship would complete me and tried remaining single, I simply substituted one idol for another. I was unknowingly living with the regret of not going off to college and obtaining a degree because I became pregnant before finishing my senior year of high school. Being raised in a family where most didn't even achieve a high school diploma, I desired to be the first in my family to "make it." Those dreams were trumped when I could no longer go off to college after graduation because of the life that I was carrying inside of me due to my rebellion and refusal to abstain from sex. When you choose to have sex and produce children outside of marriage it alters your life forever.

I didn't realize it at the time because I stayed occupied, that I lived in so much regret for forfeiting a full-ride scholarship to college for motherhood at a young age. In reality, it didn't have to be that way, but it was my choices that lead me there. I remember God allowing my step-grandmother to take me to church with her from the age of about 13 and being poured into about God and what He expected of us even as children. I wish I had taken those seeds planted back then seriously and allowed the truth I was learning to guide me. I could have saved myself so much heartache and disappointment if I had.

Fast forward to after I began my walk with Christ, I would try to remain single and then I would see others in relationships and desire it again. I allowed images, which are usually only people pretending to be happy, to make me feel like I was missing out. I used to use shopping or hanging out as a coping mechanism. There is only so much shopping and debt accumulation, hanging out and being busy, and being entertained that will happen before reality begins to set in. These are examples of some of the substitutions that I struggled with, but no matter what yours are, you will learn that none of them will truly satisfy. And eventually, after the enemy sees you settled in discontentment, he will give you what you want. After receiving what I thought I needed, I saw quickly that it wasn't what I desired at all. I had to learn that nothing can take the place of God's position in our lives — that person or thing will always come up short. Your substitutions, may not have come up short just yet, I would simply say keep living, that time will surely come.

> *You must not make for yourself an idol of any kind or an image of anything in the heavens or on the earth or in the sea. You must not bow down to them or worship them, for I, the Lord your God, am a jealous God who will not tolerate your affection for any other gods. I lay the sins of the parents upon their children; the entire family is affected—even children in the third and fourth generations of those who reject me.*
> *—Exodus 20:4–5 (NLT)*

Chapter 9
CHOICES BRING CHANGES

Now what's even crazier is after choosing wrong, the light bulb still didn't come on. When we hear "light bulb" automatically, we think of common-sense things or the idea that would produce the best outcome. In my carnal mind, the solution was to move out and get my own place with my new family, but I didn't understand the doors that I was opening. Now, just as those who went before me did, I made the choice to move in with my then-boyfriend, and we would be this happy family. That was a lie, this was just the beginning of more heartache, and it even opened the door for physical abuse. Can you believe that at one point I really convinced myself that a man hitting you was a sign of his love towards you? Stupid right? Yet, it's the reality of so many broken women. Before you know it the "accidental" hit turns into a part of your life.

Over the years I've heard so many judgments made on this topic, but one could never truly understand unless you have walked in those shoes. I will say that it is for this purpose that we have to understand Who love is and be fully persuaded that real love would never cause this type of pain. I would urge any woman going through the things I endured to run for her life to the safety of Christ! Fortunately for me, I was able to escape it without death being the outcome, but there are so many who aren't alive now to say the same. After a while I believe every person will get tired of going through a situation like that, I sure did!

There is a sad misconception that in order to learn something, you must go through the experience to know better. I believe that we are surrounded by so many who have made certain choices, and we can learn not to choose the same by their experience. It's so simple, if my sister placed her hand in a fire and was burned, it shouldn't take me placing my hand in it as well for me to know that I'll get burned. Likewise, we see cycles and behaviors around us, and we choose the same and get the same result or deal with worse. Understand that with every choice, the entire course of your life can be altered and can affect everyone connected to you. I will end with this, choose wisely!

Chapter 10
THE PROMISED HARVEST

Honestly, growing tired was just the fulfillment of what God promises in His word, which is if we sow in the flesh, of the flesh we will reap corruption (Galatians 6:8). Abuse is a part of the corruption that comes in choosing wrong relationships that God never intended for us. It also shows that though there may be temporary moments of happiness in those situations, you could never find true joy and contentment.

So fast forward, five years after my oldest son was born, my romantic relationship began to dwindle in the natural, but I didn't know that in the midst of all the chaos, God was setting me up to shipwreck what I had been calling life, to push me into His purpose that He had planned for me all along. Don't get me wrong, in no way am I saying that God authored any of these situations because it was truly my choices and the choices of others, but He has a way of turning man's craziness into glory! The only difference was now the shift in the promise! Up to this point, though I desired to reap happiness and true love, I didn't realize that the ground that I was sowing in couldn't produce that.

Due to rebellion, there were promises of consequences for disobedience, and trust me, there were many that I endured. Honestly, a lot of things that culture calls normal ups and downs are really just consequences that we endure when we operate outside of God. When I chose to do relationships without including or consulting God, I was moving blindly and being led blindly, and the word of God has an expected end for this — a ditch. Likewise, after surrendering my life to Christ there was a new expectation of promises. When we hear about God's promises, our carnal mind usually goes straight to material things, but the most important promises that God desires to give to us will be internal, starting with being filled with the Holy Spirit.

My question would then be this: Have you been trying to build something that you aren't quite getting the results that you desired or expected? Have you been feeling like you have been giving your all in a situation and keep coming up empty? Does it sometimes feel like no matter how much you try, you can never seem to find yourself out of the same place, and you're constantly dealing with the same issues? If that's you, I tell you the truth that what you are experiencing is the product of sowing into a ground that isn't able to produce the type of harvest that you desire. Or perhaps you are following someone that may not have the proper map that could lead to success. I would also encourage you to begin to pursue the One (Jesus), who knows all things, so that He may guide you into getting the best outcome for your life. He is no liar, and what His word promises comes true! Maybe it's time to start investigating what His word says and applying it that you may find yourself on the right side of His promises.

Let them alone. They are blind leaders of the blind. And if the blind leads the blind, both will fall into a ditch.
—Matthew 15:14 (NKJV)

Then Peter said to them, "Repent, and let every one of you be baptized in the name of Jesus Christ for the remission

*of sins; and you shall receive the gift of the Holy Spirit.
For the promise is to you and to your children, and to all
who are afar off, as many as the Lord our God will call."*
—*Acts 2:38–39 (NKJV)*

*For he who sows to his flesh will of the flesh reap
corruption, but he who sows to the Spirit will of the Spirit
reap everlasting life.*
 —*Galatians 6:8 (NKJV)*

*For if we sin willfully after we have received the
knowledge of the truth, there no longer remains a
sacrifice for sins, but a certain fearful expectation of
judgment, and fiery indignation which will devour the
adversaries.*
—*Hebrews 10:26–27 (NKJV)*

Chapter 11
PURSUIT

Looking back, I would have never pictured me being where I am now and my life being the way it is. After pursuing other things and coming up short every time, I finally allowed God to bring me to the end of myself. The definition of insanity is doing the same thing and expecting a different result, so I knew it was time for something different. At this time, I was now a mother of three, and what I thought was there to destroy me was what God was using to make me free. I was relationship free, my oldest was 5, and the twins were about to be 6 months, and the Lord moved us to Port St. Lucie, Florida — a quiet town far enough away from the things that were familiar.

The crazy part is that sometimes we believe that moving one location to another is the change we need, but the reality is if you don't let God change who you are, you will be the same you but just in a new place. Thank God He didn't allow me to remain the same. Not even a week after relocating God used my cousin and his wife to lead me to Christ. I still remember walking up to the altar after the gospel was preached, and my heart was pricked and ready to repent and change. I remember asking for forgiveness and calling on the name of Jesus and falling into His loving arms of grace — literally!

That was just the beginning of my pursuit of Christ! Up until then, it was just Him pursuing after me and drawing me to Himself. I would love to say that everything was perfect after that day and that I never erred again, but that wouldn't be true. Though my sins were forgiven, there was still a process that I had to endure that was up ahead that I didn't know at the time would be the fight of my life. A lot of times, we believe that the altar is where it ends, but in reality, it is the place where we then become the offering to God through Christ. It is where we leave our old nature and way of doing things and take on the mind of Christ and His ways.

I'll tell you now, our old nature in sin is completely contrary to that. My advice would be to throw out everything you think you know, especially if it doesn't line up with the word of God and begin to learn of Him. Don't assume you know God, because if we did, there are paths we wouldn't have taken and choices we wouldn't have made had we truly known who He is. To pursue Him sounds complicated but look at it like this: when we were in sin and pursuing after a man, we wanted to know everything about them and what pleased them, and once we learned what those things were, we moved quickly to do them. It's the same with God, only we learn who He is and what He desires through His word (the Holy Bible).

> *Study this Book of Instruction continually. Meditate on it day and night so you will be sure to obey everything written in it. Only then will you prosper and succeed in all you do.*
> —*Joshua 1:8 (NLT)*

Seek the Kingdom of God above all else, and live righteously, and he will give you everything you need.
—Matthew 6:33 (NLT)

Chapter 12
FOUNDATION

My first two years of salvation, I remember reading my Bible a lot; it was so interesting to me, and honestly, as a Daughter, it always should be. When you find yourself being weaned away from the word, it's time to check your heart and see where the shift has taken place. A perfect analogy is that just as we need food to eat for our natural nourishment, we need the word of God to be spiritually nourished.

Picture your spirit as a giant, the more you feed it, the bigger it grows, and likewise, the less you nourish it, the weaker it becomes. A common thing I hear people say when it comes to reading the word is, "I don't understand the Bible." Let me clear this up for you, without Holy Spirit, understanding the Bible is like an only English-speaking person trying to understand a foreign language. So when you have chosen this path of TRUTH and pursuing God through Jesus Christ and have repented of your sins and asked Christ into your heart, you must ask Him to fill you with His precious Holy Spirit.

So if you sinful people know how to give good gifts to your children, how much more will your heavenly Father give the Holy Spirit to those who ask him.

When you think about a foundation in the natural sense, you visualize the bottom frame of a house or structure that an entire building is built upon. The only problem comes when that foundation isn't built properly, and in turn, it leaves all other parts of the structure susceptible to destruction. Likewise, in the faith, Christ has to be the foundation. His life, death, and resurrection are the foundation of the Christian faith! The word Christian in itself simply means "Christ-like." This is so important because we are living in a time where the word of God and His standards in Christ are being built on man's opinion and preference and not the truth of the word of God.

> *For Jesus is the one referred to in the Scriptures, where it says, 'The stone that you builders rejected has now become the cornerstone.' There is salvation in no one else! God has given no other name under heaven by which we must be saved.*
> *—Acts 4:11–12 (NLT)*

The Bible even talks about a great falling away that will take place in the earth, where the believers will begin to fall away from Christ! Looking at the things that are actually happening, I can see that this is manifesting in doctrine. People are seeking after God and beginning to mix the word of God with culture, opinions, and man's religion, and in turn, so many are left confused. With confusion, there is no room for victory, and in turn, people are discouraged and turn away from the faith or get lured into strange doctrines that don't lead to life.

Now the Holy Spirit tells us clearly that in the last times some will turn away from the true faith; they will follow deceptive spirits and teachings that come from demons. These people are hypocrites and liars, and their consciences are dead. They will say it is wrong to be married and wrong to eat certain foods. But God created those foods to be eaten with thanks by faithful people who know the truth.
—1 Timothy 4:1–3 (NLT)

With those things in mind, it is crucial that when you begin your relationship with God through Christ you begin to read the word of God. You will need teachers and tutors to train you in the word as well, who will watch out for your soul. But even then, weigh the things you are being taught to the word.

Work hard so you can present yourself to God and receive his approval. Be a good worker, one who does not need to be ashamed and who correctly explains the word of truth.
—2 Timothy 2:15 (NLT)

And I will give you shepherds after my own heart, who will guide you with knowledge and understanding.
—Jeremiah 3:15 (NLT)

You have been taught the holy Scriptures from childhood, and they have given you the wisdom to receive the salvation that comes by trusting in Christ Jesus. All Scripture is inspired by God and is useful to teach us what is true and to make us realize what is wrong in our lives. It corrects us when we are wrong and teaches us to do

what is right. God uses it to prepare and equip his people to do every good work.
— 2 Timothy 3:15–17 (NLT)

Let us think of ways to motivate one another to acts of love and good works. And let us not neglect our meeting together, as some people do, but encourage one another, especially now that the day of his return is drawing near.
— Hebrews 10:24–25 (NLT)

I'll end this chapter with this, there is no relationship with God without Jesus Christ, and there is no fellowship with Jesus without God's word. He is the living word! Let no one deceive you that:

- You don't need to go to church
- You don't need to read the Bible
- The Bible is written by man so you shouldn't trust it
- The Bible is used to control you, etc.

The word of God is made available to make us more like Christ and to prepare and equip us for life in this world and the one to come.

Chapter 13
IN SPIRIT AND IN TRUTH

He is so amazing! The Bible refers to Him as the One who will be your HELPER, FRIEND, CONVICTER of sins, and LEADER into all truth, to name a few. The greatest of them all to identify Him as is The SEAL, so picture Him as the glue that holds us in unity with the Lord. We live in a time where people are calling a lot of things "holy" or "God" that don't line up with the word. Though someone can fall under the power of Holy Spirit, that isn't necessarily the evidence that Holy Spirit is present, nor is speaking in tongues. I say this not to discredit either, but to clarify so that you don't let what you see or hear be the sole factors to convince you that Holy Spirit is at work.

Holy Spirit will empower you to live a holy life that pleases God. So how will you know if Holy Spirit is present? You believe it by faith after you ask, seek, and knock, and the evidence is that you will see a change in you. Like me, your change may not be instant in some areas though it can be if you believe, one thing's for sure, you will no longer be comfortable doing the things you use to do. There's a shift that takes place in your heart, and when you begin to move in a way that isn't like God you will know. I would say listen to that "tugging" on your heart, don't resist it because He is only trying to lead you to true freedom. Don't be surprised when HE couples that tug with the word because He desires that you see how He sees things.

The next important thing is that you understand that the things that God is revealing to you, you are now accountable for. Meaning, your Father doesn't want you to only hear and see how He views things, but as a child, He desires you to hear and follow instructions. And not just for that day but for the rest of the days you are allowed to live on earth. The beauty is if we do mess up, we can come to Him with our mess-ups, and He is faithful to forgive us. We may not be perfect, but we daily strive towards perfection in Christ and to meet the measure that God desires for us. We did enough things in the world independent of the guidance and direction of God. And in Christ, the course of direction is simplified through Holy Spirit.

I also want to add that being filled with the Spirit of God is important because outside of Him we can't please God. Without pleasing God, my friend, there is no Christianity or faith. The word tells us that without Holy Spirit, we don't belong to God; when was the last time you heard that preached? If having Him is that crucial, don't you think that this is the knowledge that should be shared in the church? Well whether you've heard it before or not, you just read it here, so make asking Him to live in you a priority!

> *For the sinful nature is always hostile to God. It never did obey God's laws, and it never will. That's why those who are still under the control of their sinful nature can never please God.*
> *—Romans 8:7–8 (NLT)*

> *And I will ask the Father, and he will give you another Advocate, who will never leave you. He is the Holy Spirit,*

who leads into all truth. The world cannot receive him, because it isn't looking for him and doesn't recognize him. But you know him, because he lives with you now and later will be in you.
  —John 14:16–17 (NLT)

And when He has come, He will convict the world of sin, and of righteousness, and of judgment.
—John 16:8 (NKJV)

But you are not in the flesh but in the Spirit, if indeed the Spirit of God dwells in you. Now if anyone does not have the Spirit of Christ, he is not His.
—Romans 8:9 (NKJV)

However, when He, the Spirit of truth, has come, He will guide you into all truth; for He will not speak on His own authority, but whatever He hears He will speak; and He will tell you things to come.
  —John 16:13 (NKJV)

Chapter 14
CONSISTENCY

I can honestly say this is an area that I have struggled with the most, being consistent! We live in a time where there are many behaviors that are repetitious for us that are not productive or that lack the ability to add any true value to our lives. For example, one may spend a lot of time investing in watching television and social media which, can be a huge distraction, and a lot of times work against any true progress in your life. Imagine shifting that time and dedication to something that could help build you as a person, both naturally and spiritually! I think as a believer, one of the things that you will have to work the hardest at is being consistent in the things of God. As a believer, it is not an optional thing to read the word, pray, worship and praise, fast, and seek the Lord. The problem is sometimes these things are treated as though they are.

Take it one day at a time! Do today what you know to do and trust the rest to the Lord to lead and guide you in the way you should go! Then I would say don't look forward to this drastic transformation all at once, remember you are in a process that continues until Jesus returns. However, expect fruit! The fruit is simply evidence of the change that has taken place in your heart. I can promise this: when you make it a daily goal to be consistent in the things of God, not just to do another task on your checklist, but to truly get to know Him, you will see the changes.

Continue listening to the voice of God, reading your Bible, praying, and being obedient to the word you know. Remember, Holy Spirit will be your guide and help you along the journey, so you won't have to do it alone. Religion is simply repeating the same thing continually. Though I am not fond of this word in Christendom because it is all about relationship, believers need to develop a religion in studying the word of God and practicing the things of God. It is in the repetition that victory and growth are found. Don't be one of those people who try following Christ as a fad, and when they get bored, fall away. I pray that you delight in doing the things of God, and in return, the Father finds His delight in you!

> *For you were once darkness, but now you are light in the Lord. Walk as children of light (for the fruit of the Spirit is in all goodness, righteousness, and truth), finding out what is acceptable to the Lord. And have no fellowship with the unfruitful works of darkness, but rather expose them. For it is shameful even to speak of those things which are done by them in secret. But all things that are exposed are made manifest by the light, for whatever makes manifest is light.*
> *—Ephesians 5:8–13 (NKJV)*

> *Work hard so you can present yourself to God and receive his approval. Be a good worker, one who does not need to be ashamed and who correctly explains the word of truth.*
> *—2 Timothy 2:15 (NLT)*

Chapter 15
IT'S PART OF THE PROCESS

In this process, God has shown me so many ugly truths about myself, and it is honestly hard at times to stand before the mirror of His word. We sometimes convince ourselves that we are victims or that we are good, but when we see ourselves apart from Christ, we truly see how wrong we are. I remember blaming the guys that I dated for not being who I believed they were supposed to be, but truth is, my life never belonged to me anyway to even think it was okay to just allow anyone in it. I had to realize that every time I allowed someone in the door of my life without God's permission or direction, I was in violation. Some would argue that it is in those experiences that we learn the most, right? Wrong! That way of thinking was ok when I was in the world and did things according to my own desires, but now He is in control.

> *But you are not in the flesh but in the Spirit, if indeed the Spirit of God dwells in you. Now if anyone does not have the Spirit of Christ, he is not His.*
> *—Romans 8:9 (NKJV)*

To be honest, a lot of the bitterness and anger that I held on to for so many years came from me blaming other people for the bad choices I made. Don't get me wrong, some things happen in our lives that we can't control, but there is always a time where we shift to making choices. Unfortunately, some of those choices are made after heartbreaks or wounds have been inflicted, but it is our job to give that wounded heart to God and truly allow Him to heal and fix the brokenness. I sometimes wonder how things could have been different if I had just given all over to God from the beginning, like at the first sight of trouble, just run to Him and stayed there. Thank God I don't have to spend my life wondering and wandering; I can now know because I am connected to the One who knows all things.

> *The LORD is near to those who have a broken heart, And*
> *saves such as have a contrite spirit.*
> —*Psalm 34:18 (NKJV)*

God never just shows us what's wrong with us. He gives us the solution — He *is* the solution! It was never in His plans for us to be hurt and broken and used and abused, but when we as people begin to choose apart from Him and take control of our own lives, we open the door to disfunction. Who wants to continue walking around blind when you have the ability to see clearly? That's exactly what Christ is to us. He becomes the lamp that lights our path, so we don't have to make choices blindly any longer. I know this can be hard for many because we are so used to not having to answer to anyone or just simply doing what we want. The truth is, it was this way of handling things that got most of us in the trouble we were in because we had no accountability. Don't get me wrong, you will make mistakes, but get familiar with changing, learning, and growing because it is a part of God's process!

Your word is a lamp to my feet and a light to my path.
—Psalm 119:105 (NKJV)

Chapter 16
ACCOUNTABILITY

Accountability is a good thing! I had to say that because when most people hear that word the first thing that comes to mind is "people in your business." Let's clear this up, in the Kingdom, isolation is a trap! It is a tool of the enemy to keep your life in secrecy so that there is no one around to be a voice of Godly reason. Therefore, everything you choose to do alone is usually governed by your own sense of right or wrong, and a lot of times, that is contrary to the word of God. God designed the body of Christ for a reason, that we wouldn't have to do this walk alone. A sheep wandering alone is easy prey for a fox, don't be easy prey!

> *Where there is no counsel, the people fall; But in the multitude of counselors there is safety.*
> *—Proverbs 11:14 (NKJV)*

> *A man who isolates himself seeks his own desire; He rages against all wise judgment. A fool has no delight in understanding, But in expressing his own heart.*
> *—Proverbs 18:1–2 (NKJV)*

Surround yourself with people who will help you grow in Christ. I'm so grateful for the people God has placed around me to help develop me into the woman He has called me to be. I will say this, I didn't always like people in my business, and honestly, there are times where I desire to retreat from the community of believers that have been given to me, but I'm thankful for the brethren that help keep me in position. I have had arguments with some, there were times I disagreed with and disliked some, but I've learned that these were all opportunities for me to be trained in and grow in the love of God. God was designing situations for me to be changed to look more like HIm.

Looking back, I see most of the problems that I had with others were summed up in me trying to prove that "I'm right," when the heart of the Father is to pursue peace. I'm learning and growing daily, and it is the relationships that God has placed me in that are training me in righteousness. Don't push away the people that God is placing around you because there are things that God wants to do for and in you, with their assistance. It doesn't mean that things will always be perfect but grow in love and remain open to who the Lord wants to add or remove from your life. It may be you who needs the word of encouragement from a friend today, but it may be them tomorrow, we all need each other so GROW!

Depart from evil and do good; Seek peace and pursue it.
—Psalm 34:14 (NKJV)

And He Himself gave some to be apostles, some prophets, some evangelists, and some pastors and teachers, for the equipping of the saints for the work of ministry, for the edifying of the body of Christ, till we all come to the unity of the faith and of the knowledge of the Son of God, to a perfect man, to the measure of the stature of the fullness of Christ; that we should no longer be children, tossed to

and fro and carried about with every wind of doctrine, by the trickery of men, in the cunning craftiness of deceitful plotting, but, speaking the truth in love, may grow up in all things into Him who is the head—Christ—from whom the whole body, joined and knit together by what every joint supplies, according to the effective working by which every part does its share, causes growth of the body for the edifying of itself in love.
—Ephesians 4:11–16 (NKJV)

Just as a body, though one, has many parts, but all its many parts form one body, so it is with Christ. For we were all baptized by one Spirit so as to form one body—whether Jews or Gentiles, slave or free—and we were all given the one Spirit to drink. Even so the body is not made up of one part but of many.

Now if the foot should say, "Because I am not a hand, I do not belong to the body," it would not for that reason stop being part of the body. And if the ear should say, "Because I am not an eye, I do not belong to the body," it would not for that reason stop being part of the body. If the whole body were an eye, where would the sense of hearing be? If the whole body were an ear, where would the sense of smell be? But in fact God has placed the parts in the body, every one of them, just as he wanted them to be. If they were all one part, where would the body be? As it is, there are many parts, but one body.

The eye cannot say to the hand, "I don't need you!" And the head cannot say to the feet, "I don't need you!" On the contrary, those parts of the body that seem to be

weaker are indispensable, and the parts that we think are less honorable we treat with special honor. And the parts that are unpresentable are treated with special modesty, while our presentable parts need no special treatment. But God has put the body together, giving greater honor to the parts that lacked it, so that there should be no division in the body, but that its parts should have equal concern for each other. If one part suffers, every part suffers with it; if one part is honored, every part rejoices with it.
—1 Corinthians 12:12–26 (NKJV)

I know that may have been a lot of verses to take in, but because I understand that relating to people should be our strength as human beings, it literally is one of the greatest struggles. For that reason, I'd rather not give my reasoning or experiences, but the word of God which will not change. God has a lot to say about how we relate to one another, but the problem is, so does everyone else. I'd rather listen to the words of the One that created us, though.

Chapter 17
WAIT ON THE LORD

I know some of you are reading this and are like, ok, this is good so far, but let's get to the deets on your relationship status. That's easy! I am simply married to Christ! A lot of people wonder what that means exactly. It means that when I accepted Christ, not only did HE become my Lord and Savior, but I also become His bride. My life no longer belongs to me, but I am now submitted and committed to Him and His plans for my life. With that being said, I have no time to be dating or testing the waters because my affections belong to God while I'm single. Not only that, but according to the word, a wife is found, not seeking for her husband. I know our culture has accepted the pursuing woman mentality, but that was never God's design.

Do not fear, for you will not be ashamed;
Neither be disgraced, for you will not be put to shame;
For you will forget the shame of your youth,
And will not remember the reproach of your widowhood
anymore.
For your Maker is your husband,
The Lord of hosts is His name;
And your Redeemer is the Holy One of Israel;
He is called the God of the whole earth.

For the Lord has called you
Like a woman forsaken and grieved in spirit,
Like a youthful wife when you were refused,"
Says your God.
"For a mere moment I have forsaken you,
But with great mercies I will gather you.
With a little wrath I hid My face from you for a moment;
But with everlasting kindness I will have mercy on you,"
Says the Lord, your Redeemer.
—Isaiah 54:4–8 (NKJV)

But I want you to be without care. He who is unmarried
cares for the things of the Lord—how he may please the
Lord. But he who is married cares about the things of the
world—how he may please his wife. There is a difference
between a wife and a virgin. The unmarried woman cares
about the things of the Lord, that she may be holy both in
body and in spirit. But she who is married cares about the
things of the world—how she may please her husband.
—1 Corinthians 7:32–34 (NKJV)

He who finds a wife finds a good thing, and obtains favor
from the LORD.
—Proverbs 18:22 (NKJV)

That last scripture is often quoted but, not many give attention to the detail of what it implies. How can a man want to marry someone that he finds that is already a wife? Being a wife means she is already devoted to someone else, which in the average person's mind would mean there is no room for another. This wife that is implied to have been found in this verse is referring to a woman like myself who has postured herself in devotion to the Lord, and any true man of God won't mind sharing her with Him. A lot of women are wondering why they aren't being found, and it's mainly because, in a lot of cases, we are postured as girlfriends or postured in the friend zone of someone who doesn't deem you to be wife material. I have, on so many occasions, been found positioned just as I stated, but thank God for a renewed mind. Now I simply won't allow someone to come and block the view of the one who my Father will one day send.

I do desire marriage, I'm just not willing to compromise who I am as a Daughter or settle for less than God's best for me. Even greater than that, I won't be distracted from the purpose that God has on my life to start pursuing something that God never designed for me to be pursuing. I can't begin to tell you of the time that I have wasted concerning myself with marriage, at times where God was still working on me. I wanted God to add to me what I thought I was missing, but it turns out everything I needed I already had! It's as simple as this, if God has not given you a spouse yet, you don't need it yet! When the need arises, just as with everything else, He will meet that need.

> *Therefore do not be like them. For your Father knows the things you have need of before you ask Him.*
> *— Matthew 6:8 (NKJV)*

Chapter 18
A CALL TO PURITY

S omebody right now is saying, "I have desires, and they need to be met." I say, Sis, it's those desires that have led us to destruction and disappointment in the past — I know they have for me! Its time to allow God to nail those fleshly desires to the cross and allow Him to purify you so that your desires become what He desires. You are now the temple of the Holy Spirit, there is no room for the old you and the you that you are becoming to coexist. It's not that you will never have another ungodly desire again, but now you can bring those thoughts in alignment with TRUTH!

I always tell women, "Don't put any confidence in your flesh." Those aren't my words, but they are sourced from the word and so true! It was in the times when I thought I was strong, where my flesh showed me I was wrong. A part of purity is understanding that outside of the strength of God (the willing Spirit), this flesh is weak, and if we give it room to thrive, it will do just that! I go so far as to not share my number with guys unless it's for other purposes like ministry or work, but even then, I set boundaries. I don't talk long hours or late at night! I know it sounds childish, but I am a child, a child of God! No, but seriously, it was following little principles like these that have helped me walk in victory for years now from fornication! I'm not boasting in myself at all, but in the fact that submitting to the word of God has proven to be effective in my life.

> *For I know that in me (that is, in my flesh) nothing good dwells; for to will is present with me, but how to perform what is good I do not find.*
> *—Romans 7:18 (NKJV)*

> *Therefore submit to God. Resist the devil and he will flee from you.*
> *—James 4:7 (NKJV)*

> *Catch all the foxes, those little foxes, before they ruin the vineyard of love, for the grapevines are blossoming!*
> *—Song of Solomon 2:15 (NLT)*

You don't have to worry about the vines being destroyed in your life if you kill the small foxes. Also, purity is about more than just not having sex; it's your mindset and behavior that simply desires to please God. It's understanding that you are the temple of God and not being willing to defile His temple. I say it like this, purity is the Daughters portion! Again, I'll say it, this is not an overnight process, and following this way will get you mocked and persecuted. As the word says, "the sufferings of this present time are not worthy to be compared to the glory that will be revealed in us" (Romans 8:18). As spectators watch you get the victory and overcome the things that use to keep you bound, they will start asking what's your secret? Then you too can tell them the good news of how the Lord brought you through!

Don't you realize that your body is the temple of the Holy Spirit, who lives in you and was given to you by God? You do not belong to yourself.
— 1 Corinthians 6:19 (NLT)

God blesses those whose hearts are pure, for they will see God.
— Matthew 5:8 (NLT)

Run from anything that stimulates youthful lusts. Instead, pursue righteous living, faithfulness, love, and peace. Enjoy the companionship of those who call on the Lord with pure hearts.
— 2 Timothy 2:22 (NLT)

Chapter 19
ENDURANCE IS KEY

I've been through so much in this walk so far, but the key I'm learning is to endure. Everything I talked about so far will get hard at some point. There will be times you will be discouraged and want to give up, but in those moments, continue to press. Keep running the race of faith in God, and you will see mountains move in your life and doors being opened for you that you never imagined were possible. Don't just view that in a materialistic way either because Christ in you is the glory that the Father desires to come forth, and when HE does it, He wants you to use it to help other people.

> *Therefore, since we are surrounded by such a huge crowd of witnesses to the life of faith, let us strip off every weight that slows us down, especially the sin that so easily trips us up. And let us run with endurance the race God has set before us. We do this by keeping our eyes on Jesus, the champion who initiates and perfects our faith. Because of the joy awaiting him, he endured the cross, disregarding its shame. Now he is seated in the place of honor beside God's throne. Think of all the hostility he endured from sinful people; then you won't become weary and give up.*
> *—Hebrews 12:1-3 (NLT)*

But the one who endures to the end will be saved.
—Matthew 24:13 (NLT)

I would have never thought that I would be entrusted with a ministry to empower women in the same areas that the enemy used to overtake me in. I would have never dreamed that I would value myself and know my worth when I come from a background of being promiscuous. Who would have thought that the young girl who had mistaken the identity of the father of her first child, would live holy? Yes, I've experienced that too! It comes with the territory of promiscuity. I could have never dreamed of being used to preach the gospel of Jesus with this same mouth that used to utter such wicked things. I didn't even know I had the gift of poetry or to write pieces that would bring glory to God while inspiring others on their journey to freedom. I didn't know that I had books inside of me, that's why today these words you can read!

I give all glory and honor to God for my new life in Christ! Before you know it, you will look around and your whole life will be transformed by truth and you'll be what God already knew you could be — a Daughter After Truth Every day!

Don't copy the behavior and customs of this world, but let God transform you into a new person by changing the way you think. Then you will learn to know God's will for you, which is good and pleasing and perfect.
—Romans 12:2 (NLT)

www.ingramcontent.com/pod-product-compliance
Lightning Source LLC
LaVergne TN
LVHW051817080426
835513LV00017B/1994